DANCE THROUGH
THE CENTURY

A Suffolk Life

Joyce Barton

Dance Through the Century

A Suffolk Life

First published in 2003
by
Mousehold Press, Norwich
for
Joyce Barton

Front cover photograph: Sue Mullard

ISBN 1-874739-31-5

Printed by CopyTECH (UK), Peterborough

PRE-WAR
LATE THIRTIES

HEATHER HONEY

How many lovers have lain on this common land,
Deep in the heather and low in the ling,
Braked from the breeze by the whispering birch tree,
Plighting their troth with a kiss for a ring?

Can the dark gorse tell the number of maidens
Who saw where the gold shone, nor looked on the thorn;
Who lavished their love, as the heather its honey,
On the wandering pirates who seize in half-scorn?

Let the grey clouds dredge their curtain above them,
Let the smooth grass spring again from their feet;
Passed is the youth, the desire and the memory,
The sunshine is glancing, the moment was sweet.

PURGATORY

Where the dark shades of night draw down to meet the level
    land, they lie,
The curious creatures, sunken souls, with no respite or
    destiny,
In the groping half-light misted with the air of yesterday,
Ne'er forgetting, only sorrowing, blindly following, they cry.

Behind them, like a map revealing, warmly spread the haunts
    of men,
But before them – blank, unheeding, every yearning, ever
    needing,
Aching wounds for ever bleeding –
Dip the purgatorial deeps, the sea whose shores they cannot scan.

Coldly blow the winds and rawly, crevice-piercing, singing shrill,
Centuries undisciplined, unmodified by heart's goodwill,
And the no-men tremble moaning,
And the waters wreak their will.

SONG OF THE UNSOPHISTICATED

I love the country for its hedges,
Their inaccuracy of line;
The cities have their clear-cut edges,
Their serried ranks of window ledges,
Perspectively precise skyscrapers:
I love the country where light-vapours
Cloud uncertainly the ragged pine.

The country roads wind gladly free
Of close-set kerb or pavement plane;
And individuality
Speaks artlessly from plant and tree.
In city parks the flowers grow
With care and nurture two by two,
Much tidier than a lane.

There's wastage in the brown fields
Of fruits men fail to gather,
The shelter that the town yields
Is absent from the Down wealds;
But Nature's flowing sweetness
Ousts all artificial neatness –
Of her unhampered rhythm I would rather.

So I will to the country, and live where men may sing
Of the bounty of the Autumn and the miracle of Spring.

A SUPPLICATIO

Help Thou my unbelief O God,
Who need, but have not faith to p
Who cannot tell if from the sod
We rise to face another day
On some far planet, and forget
The loves and ills of this brief world:
Or if, when here our star is set,
Each personality is furled
And folded in an ordained whole.
Lord God, how can I pray, who doubt
The existence of a separate soul;
And probe the written word, e'en flout
The view that Jesus was divine?
Good God, I need the peace of prayer,
Give me a sign.

TO OUR OLD AGE

When the jaded days have massed and merged
Into years when loves turn likes;
When aging steps are singly urged,
Before the long dark strikes;
When our shrunken bodies shrink away
From pleasures then dubbed sour,
And our crabbed minds hark to yesterday:
Remember this one hour.

When the slow blood courses sluggishly,
And the cold hands clutch for heat;
When the shuffling steps turn childishly
To the nearest sunny seat:
Gaze on the unchanging sun above,
And think, from your old decline,
How the white fire of your young love
Burnt with the red of mine.

WAR
1939-45

UTILITY LAND

The lark that scales and beats his
    wings against the gates of God,
Is calling in hysteria from
    meadows turned to clod,
Importuning Providence to spare
    his home from plough –
For this denizen of secret grass
    is in the army now.

Acre after acre drilled and
    spawning wheat,
Luscious miles of grazing land
    laid waste that men may eat;
The flower' roots are mangled,
    in vain the lark may soar –
The cowslips and the buttercups
    are casualties of war.

DAYLIGHT ATTACK

Hear the heavy bombers groaning,
hesitating on their mark,
As the anti-aircraft barrage sweeps their course,
a splintered arc,
Rocks the earth and shudders houses.
Listen to the whine of weight,
To the loaded iron dropping –
all the raiders' ugly freight.
Hear the smash and feel the blasting,
steel your nerves and choke the scream:
Somewhere in that sobbing silence
souls now learn what mortals dream.

Listen to the hungry crackling
rising from a well of fire,
whence the angry flames lace turret,
blacken buttress, lap the spire:
Watch the hollow crater gaping
where the shelter should appear,
Harbouring its herded inmates,
young in age but old in fear.
See the covered shattered bodies, little children sacrificed:
While a blue Madonna ponders on a wooden wounded Christ.

VIGIL

I am afraid in the night,
In the dark night
When the shadows join hands.
You lie beside me, still, asleep,
You arm heavy with unconsciousness
And your breathing laboured because you are greatly tired.
I can see you My Love, My Beloved:
Your hair is dark on the pillow
And your face in sleep is a blur unmasking the boy I never knew.
Tonight there is no life in your limbs, my Husband;
Your sleep is heavy,
But I am awake
Thinking of death.
Only this moment is mine,
This moment before the night dissolves to day,
And you are gone.
Gone where those other men lie now, dead.
Dead.
Dead in a pit of black wound and red pain,
And after the scream they breathe heavily and their limbs stiffen,
So.
And they are not John or David any more,
Only flesh to putrefy.
My Love, my Love,
This night I am afraid:

You have departed already;
And how can I turn to my God,
How can I say in my selfishness,
Deliver me, Lord, from this?
Can I beg for the battle to finish,
That must be fought?
The lips of the dead men move:
They say,
We too were loved
And why should you escape?
And God must say,
Little men, who will not learn,
This is your quarrel;
I am the Comforter.
But if comfort comes with bereavement,
Can I console myself now,
As I lie by my Love who 'sembles death,
In the dark night, afraid?

1944

TO BARRY MICHAEL JOHN

I, who agonised for thee
In Woman's own Gethsemane,
Pray, my son, that thou wilt be

Brave to never suffer wrong
Or falsehood: in temptation strong;
With others' frailty bearing long.

Yet if thou shouldst not achieve
The manly blessings I would breathe,
But fall in weakness on the hill
Of life, my son – I'll love thee still.

THE HILL

He loved the sun. Did he realise, when his
    eyes grew dim with haze,
That his eyeballs pricked by the fading beams
    showed then an opaque glaze?
Did he know, as the trill of the last clear lark
    pierced to his numbing brain,
That was the last bird he would hear, that
    he'd never hear again?
He loved the wind and the earth beneath,
    that he lies under now,
They were life and hope as he breathed and
    climbed to the conquered hilltop's brow.
He is dead and gone. The sun shines on.
    And God, I could bear it still
Though he is dead, if I knew he died
    hoping to climb his hill.

EPITAPH ON A SOLDIER

In some far field my true-love lies,
His flooded heart-blood growing cold;
The mask of death is on his eyes,
His life this day for freedom sold.

Nor will his loss remembered be,
When others desecrate the truth
In later years, except by me –
For with his passing went my youth.

INCIDENT

Away from the blood and slaughter,
Lost from my own patrol,
I lay with my face to the water
And offered the Lord my soul.

Dawn was over the forest,
The blackbird answered the owl;
Death with the day seemed surest –
My deeds of the night hung foul:
Five men pierced on my bayonet,
Strangers to me before;
They retched with the rip of their own live flesh
And sank in their own red gore.

I was a spirit of darkness,
Caged in flesh I abhorred;
The Devil was all about me,
So I took my soul to the Lord.

Mad was I in the small hours,
But cold and sane with the day;
Lost and weary and hopeless
By my enemy's well I lay,

Faint to the pit of my stomach:
She came with cautious tread
And knelt in the leaves beside me
And bathed the blood off my head.

She was my enemy's daughter,
I had killed her breed;
She offered me bread and water
And left, her flock to feed,

Knowing that I would leave her,
No mark or sign to find;
But I think of her for ever
In the abyss of my mind.

DESERT ARMY

Tired with the weariness of never knowing,
With waiting beyond hope, itself a hollow sigh;
Drugged by the flaying sun, sands ever-flowing,
Belittled by a land that gives the lie
To all man's vanities and his material –
A breath of wind will clog the whole machine,
The driver blind – the air in form ethereal
Will mirage and delude with greener scene:
How blue the sky! How brown these granite faces,
Man-moulded now that left home boyish bland;
Their white teeth flash in humourless grimaces,
Resembling live the skulls beneath the sand.
This is their graveyard who had nothing left
In life but courage. Mourn them, ye bereft.

THE CHOSEN PEOPLE

Great God of Hosts, Thy people perish!
Witness now our anguish, Lord!
Of all time most persecuted,
See, we perish by the sword.
Christ the man said, High Jehovah,
Thou wouldst mark the sparrows' fall:
Mark Thou then, and plan Thy vengeance
On the race that spreads our pall!
For we die in tens of thousands –
God, what penitence is this?
No man's sin may pay so dearly –
A noose but served for Judas' kiss –
And we the innocent, Thy chosen,
Die in depths no man should know:
Thou All-wise, All-great Jehovah
Shield us living from this blow.
Hypocrites, the Nazarene said,
When our fathers served Thy rites:
Even he, Lord, cleared the Temple,

13

He would sicken at these sights.
They defile our holy places,
Murder, filth, and rape unite
To degrade our reverent worship;
With Thy Fire avenge our plight!
When the Christ man purified him,
In the wilderness alone,
The devil then had lands to proffer –
Now is come into his own.
And we Thy landless race, Jehovah,
Of devils' spite unwilling prize,
Cry unto the God of Jacob,
Cry with bleeding, blinded eyes.
Christ the man bore crucifixion;
He was one, and we are all –
Every Hebrew stands a victim:
God, this is too bitter gall.
Thou hast seen our children butchered,
Maidens forced and young men killed,
All refinements of their torture
Suffered till our cup is filled:
And the Gentiles, Lord, will judge them,
When with no more blood to shed,
Drained of men, they cease from fighting,
To lay blood-guilt on one man's head.
On one, or few, when all are guilty –
All the Teutons' hands are red:
Deluded say – or else misguided?
Lord, they knew Thy people bled!
To tolerate sin is to act it:
Sin from sinner who will sieve?
They are all the Priest and Levite –
But Christ-led nations will forgive.
They will weigh what we have suffered,
Shall pledges be sufficient sign?
Who can speak of Retribution,
When the vengeance shall be Thine!
Champion our cause, Jehovah –
We Thy dead hosts cannot rise;
Retribute Thy peoples' sorrows!

Avenge, O Lord, the Hebrews' cries!
When we lie in Abram's bosom, Folded whole, restored
    on high:
Across the great fixed gulf, Jehovah,
Let us watch those devils die.

THE SEMPSTRESS

I saw you dead,
Above my head;
You lighted the air
Like a chandelier,
And fell with a cry
From an alien sky
With a final sound
To a foreign ground.

I sewed in my home
When you left your 'drome
(Did you say goodbye
With a merry eye?),
There was thread in my hand
When you hovered my land,
(Were you dreaming of one
Waiting on your return?):
With a song you came
To break and maim,
(But your mission turned –
'Twas yourself who burned.)

I snapt my thread;
And watched you, dead.

THERE IS A CORNER

There is a corner in a country churchyard
Where the pollen of the tall grass is shed,
A recent corner, where the staring meadow daisy
Lifts its homely head.

It is where the scythe of the verger does not reach,
And the yarrow and trefoil have their way,
That the old earth takes to herself reluctant,
And sorrow has most sway.

'Tis there that the new wooden crosses crowd together,
Where the grave-flowers are most fresh;
The tombs and the vaults tell of venerable dying,
But these clave to the flesh.

They breathed full-lunged of the air of the morning,
And kissed and cursed and were gone;
Without much glory they humbly did their duty,
And saluted death when he won.

Some halted home to die in an hour or two,
Or dead, proved a comrade's loyal care:
There they lie, all that is left of them,
Whose purpose still fights in the air.

The women weep without consolation;
The years claim measure 'ere they die,
To join in spirit the souls of the bodies
That in many country churchyards lie.

MISSING

Now the used day is folding into night,
Children are gathered home, and
    lovers love's arms seek;
Empty are mine, and hollow my

heart's plight:
Speak to me Darling. Speak.

Now the wind dies, and at its breath
   the bird
Settles with sober chords beside
   his mate;
I cannot count the days I have
   not heard:
How long, Love, must I wait?

Robbed of reflection flowers recede
   to white,
The scented cots of temporal butterfly;
To me the resting dark brings no
   respite,
Uneasily I lie.

If love could die, with death I
   might have rest,
If life could hold me hope then
   would I fight:
With neither life nor death have
   I been blessed,
And always there is night.

TO THE YOUNGER SISTERS

Pat is dead in Africa,
Two years there has lain;
Bill & Harry, Tom & George,
All are of the slain.

Fresher blood has soaked the sod
Where Sasha fell & died;
Hans & Carl in burial bed
Their enemy beside.

Bart is dust of Java's earth
Dick sank off Malay,
Hank charred when his fortress dived,
So the records say.

Thus, & thus, & thus they passed,
Phantoms that we knew;
Sweethearts of our yesteryears,
Rosemary & rue.

See the fourteens budding up
Into light undimmed,
Song & dance & love is theirs,
Ours the graves unhymned.

We are brides of countless boys
Seas & lives away:
Sultry orchids rioting
In jungles of Cathay,

Vines that purple southern slopes,
Rich & yellow grain
Swinging in the haunted winds
Of that red Ukraine.

EAST ANGLIAN AIRFIELD

For three, nay nearly four, years now the heath
Has in its wild expanse hidden a warring heart,
And sorry raiders found that far beneath
'Mid heather and dark pine an airfield played
                              its part
To fortify our coast. Situate low it lay,
And camouflaged into the infertile moor,
Sand dun and green that verges into grey,
Confusing flyers for whom 'twas landing floor.
And pilots came to circle and to light,

18

To fuel and eat, to dance and flirt, and then
To skim and soar, receding into flight,
Some true, some faithless, many young,
                    all men.
With tender touch they rode upon the air,
With a sure hand they stalked among
                    the clouds,
And wielded lightsomely a gun-site there
To take a chance with Death. Flames were
                    their shrouds.
Then we the earthbound honoured and
                    paid awe,
And laughed with them, nor planned for
                    any morrow,
But prayed a little when their place we saw
Filled by a replica. Short time for sorrow;
Only the minute mourns its latest grief,
For heavy hearts would see a nation fall,
(So war demands for sanity's relief)
And silence came to be our heroes' pall.
We watched them go that time when
                    Britain hurled –
Alone and stubborn with a new-found faith –
Her challenge of high hope to all the world.
They were her messengers: each sudden wraith
A torch of life raised in his funeral pyre,
So other men who knew the right arose
Answering the fiery cross in righteous ire.
So came America, and they are those

Her sons, transported from the plain and range,
Who land upon the heath, sail English skies,
Till suffering Europe's agony shall change,
And they shall hear the free air clamour cries
Of victory.
Britannia and Columbia then
Shall honour each with men who fought
                    by men.

DESPAIR

I cannot write these latter days
As I have written of yore,
My pen is poised upon the phrase
Too trite for five years' war.

I cannot weep. The floodgates of my sorrow
Long since have burst their banks, their source is dry:
So much of beauty might have been our morrow,
Now only desolation dulls the eye.

And as the invalid, the long night waking,
Looks to the dawn and only tempest sees,
Over the world a bitter Peace is breaking,
That augers neither respite nor release.

I cannot write these latter days
Nor utter further cry –
I cannot mourn the mould'ring dead.
The living yet to die.

THE FIRST XMAS, NEW ERA.

I, tired housewife, bent for the farmhouse
In the raw blackness building to Xmas,
Muffled and mackintoshed, leaned on the west wind
And looked on a lorry peopled by prisoners.

They, silent aliens, were not Italians,
Swarthy full Southerners. These were blond Teutons –
Only insignia marked them not English –
A labour battalion in the land of their conquerors.

From these sprung the Storm Troops, abominable Nazis,
(They had wrought havoc and widowed young women) –
But when I saw them I suffered compassion,
With pity I looked on my enemy fallen.

Neither by whistle or laugh's invitation
Did the defeated acknowledge my presence;
But as they passed, through the open wide lorry
Turning, each measured his eyes on a woman.

Hunger stared stark in their humourless faces,
Hunger of men for my drab femininity:
And I went my way cold to the farm for a chicken
In the Christmas of peace that the great war had won.

AFRICA
1949-65

FAREWELL

Not many mornings shall I see
The white mist wreathed so smokily,
Shall see the ash tree's turgid arch,
The promised pulse in the yet-bare larch –
Why do I love the mist and rain
Who may in England not remain?

Beneath each gleaming evergreen
Hang cold the drops that lave it clean;
And clear and cold on air as ice
The robin ripples, shrill, precise –
Goodbye to blackbird and to thrush
That pierce my heart from bough and bush.

Adieu to snowdrop, aconite,
More loved because they scorn the bright
And balmy days that soak in suns,
Thin rays suffice my virgin ones:
The jasmine and the celandine
Can only in my heart be mine.

Is there some plan of Providence,
Some wider chart we cannot sense,
That takes from those that love a place
Or person, so they lose not grace?
Perhaps for this my soul may be
Saved for love in eternity:
But grant, great God who knowest best,
That I sleep in England my last long rest.

THEOLOGY

Abdul basks in the early warmth of a hot Ugandan morn,
Shaded within his duka, shop-cum-stall as is the norm.
I cannot gauge Abdul Gaffa's age,
His leathery looks belie. He has a teenage son
And, indoors, an invisible wife as Muslim wives are prone.
His parsimonious livelihood rests on his ramshackle store
Roofed in corrugated sheet
With sacking walls and rough hewn posts
All open to the street.
Cross-legged Abdul Gaffa sits rolling betel chews
To sell. Into a leaf goes the nut and a chewed brown juice exudes;
Stained pavements everywhere proclaim their popularity,
Where alcohol is forbidden and cigarettes a scarcity.
Abdul vends vegetables and fruit unwashed and raw;
Puny plantains, oranges green, mango and pawpaw:
His prime commodity, pineapples imported from neighbour state –
Sixpence for smaller sizes, shilling European's rate.
One Sunday morn I cycle past from early Christian mass
And pause to purchase a pineapple to bear home for breakfast.
"Been to church?" says Abdul, speaking more by sign,
And "Yes – you go on Friday!" I reply in mime.
My answer is augmented by Abdul's Sunday dress –
Less pristine than on Friday, but by Thursday a soiled mess.
And having little converse neither English nor Arabic,
We meditate in concert till I pay my due and exit;
Then, "One God," says Abdullah and points to the brassy sky,
And "Truly, yes!" I answer, and we part in harmony.

THE SNAKEBIRD

The Snakebird is stalking
Up and down the shamba,
By the frangipani with its fallen galaxy;
Stealthily he goosesteps,
Pausing in the long grass,
Beneath the oleander and the jacaranda tree.
The Snakebird is a grey shape
Pale as water-colour,
Lovely as an etching poised before my hedge;
Silhouetted sharply,
A shadow cut in paper,
The Snakebird is a spirit from the occult's edge.

See his wary long neck
Coiled to an es-bend;
Attenuated body and long splay feet:
Clap your hands my baby!
Run, run and shake him!
Make him less unearthly with his heavy goose flight.

BY NIGHT TRAIN TO NAIROBI. ATHI PLAIN.

Heavily I lay and brooded on a fancied mannered slight,
As the coal-sucked engine jerked us rhythmically across the night,
Till my clammy nape aroused me and I rose distressed, unslept –
Threw the window down and saw what company the carriage kept.
Followed us a lovely lantern, lit our track athwart the plain,
Dimmed the tropic stars, and with her glow washed faint the milky
wain:
Lady moon, nor lovelier a lady have I ever seen
Graciously bestowing glory by her contact, as a queen.
All below, the thorns and grasses borrowed beauty out of time –
Once before, in northern winter, did I see the like, in rime;
Not their own, the vivid etchings; theirs by grace, each silhouette,
Every shifting square uncovered there another picture yet.
More than beauty, 'twas the spirit of that breathless plain I drew,

Here lay time untampered, ages no man ever knew.
Old as Eden, aye and older, from the last upheaving start
Grass had died on grass in season, thorn had bred its counterpart.

Somewhere in that godless silence, python shivered in its sleep,
Leopard stirred and flexed and rippled off where shadows lay more deep.
Long giraffe must limberly have cantered then again made hush,
Deer and dikdik took more closely of the form of thorn and bush.
If the cactus glowed more pinkly it conveyed no moral tale –
In that land of lawless nature Aesop speaks to no avail:
The gargoyle branches sing of naught, the bloated baobab is dumb;
The noiseless people make their fetish with a primal goatskin drum.

Then the power of unrestricted nature pierced my shuttered mind,
As on wasteland moonlight's bounty had the thorn and rock refined;
And I could not hold the wonder and the beauty in my heart,
Finding room as well for slight – and so I bade the hurt depart.

TALE OF TWO LEPERS CIRCA 1953

Mbale is hot at midday,
Mbale swelters then:
I leave my car window open
(pre-air-conditioning)
To shop in Mbale's main street
Where parking's free for all;
The lepers see me coming,
"Mumma! Mumma!" they call.

Thrusting their mutilated fists
Into my window frame,
"Baksheesh Memsahib, baksheesh!" they beg,
With grey stumps tapping my name.
I give them each a 6d. coin,
Enough to buy a gin;
They sit on the steps at Saldahna's
And euphoria settles in.

Until my tender conscience pricks –
Can coins infect the skin?
And who imbibes the next snifter
From an ill-rinsed glass of gin?
I voice my concern to a doctor,
A lady honed by war:
(A lovely Hollander, "Turnips we ate
All winter in '44.")

"Probably burnt-out cases,"
She professionally said.
But I gave up dishing out sixpences
And donated bananas instead.
Though the lepers prefer sobriety's devil,
It assuages my fears of contagion's evil.
So ends my song.
Am I right or wrong?

THE CEREMONY UGANDA CIRCA 1955

How still the night.
Heat palpable enshrouds a living silence
Broken but briefly by intermittent voices of kitchen hands;
Laughter. Goodnight.
Now clouds part to unveil a moon unwieldy large
And stars so bright they seem to cast shadows –
Shadows of men, or beasts, slipping behind the thorns.
Listen, and hear, far on the hills the throbbing beat of drums.
From moon past to moon present,
Unceasing, threatening, summoning,
That pulse has pounded.
Beneath the splintered howl of a hyena
Sobs that native sound, a dancing, stamping rhythm,
Or, more eerily, jagged, asymmetric, morse talking, hill to hill:
Archaic syncopation, beating blood to blood,
The roll of sorcery.
See now, those hills made visible by points of fire.
See distantly, coaxed by a drum,

The moving orange fingers each dark figure circling the fire.

Initiation night then it must be.
Oh Africa! behind the laundered shirts, the ties, the briefcases
                                         newly acquired,
Deep in the bush another world takes precedence.
Primeval rules obtain.
This is the night.
What man attains manliness who dares not?
Assembled now pubescent boys, teenaged adolescents,
Primed by bhang and pombe, driven by drum.
Drum sound, drum pound! Dance, dance and leap the fire!
Drum deafen loud, beat heart, beat!
Your turn is now.
That rusty razor knife must prove your manhood.
Dance, dance! The stench of sweat, acid of fear,
Black smoke of fires, wails, wails of womenfolk!
Face it and do not falter.
Pain most exquisite.
Now in this 20th century come Europeans,
Invited viewers of African fortitude.
"Peeled like bananas!" gasps the 7th Day Adventist.
The white photographer faints.
The European nurse from her hygienic cell
Grimly relates of "buckets of disinfectant
Below a bench tomorrow: Not all escape infection".
But tonight is shot with lightning bolts of pain:
Tears blinked away, bitten lips, a trembling uncontained.
Then blessed oblivion drowned in hashish.
Come morrow, clad in long white gowns acquired for occasion,
The heroes process the little township.
By the Post Office, telephone exchange,
By the Police Station and sundry vans outside Indian dukas,
Barefoot, bareheaded, a line of acolytes
Tenderly holding their garments from the front.

THE SUFFOLK GARDENER

Mr Lyne, rain or fine, presents himself at ten to nine;
Emerging from his mini car with hat and anorak attired
He opens wide my terrace door and steps inside,
And if he finds me not within, with dulcet tones falsetto thin
Carols Mrs Bar ton up the stairs.
A sound precaution you'll admit
Should my soul have taken a moonlight flit.
Then thereupon, his toil decreed
To mow or plant or prune (to weed
He likes not) he sets to,
A steady pace, just keen of slow.
That is if the mower will go.
And in the prescribed ninety mins
Sustained by cake and coffee
He has shaved the sward, the cuttings binned
And Mr Lyne is off. He
Has more lawns to maim
To pay his way, renew his mini,
For benefits he will not claim.
His taciturn bachelor pride ordains
Pay and be paid. A man of honour.
If formal religion seems not his habit,
Yet he knows the source of Herodian Springs
And at Christmas gives me a chocolate Santa,
At Easter a chocolate rabbit.
Mr Lyne has no wife. His much loved Mother now deceased,
     lonely lives he.
In Robin Lyne I see of Suffolk men the epitome,
Slow, staunch and stubborn, not philandering, unromantic;
And he brings to mind the tale of World War One by mother told:
That when the piping Ladies from Hell
With bloodied bayonets overran their enemies' shell-hole –
Whom did they demand should follow and hold?
The Suffolks. A regiment of Lynes.

THE COMPASSIONATE COUNTRYMAN

Above the sleepy market town, perhaps alive in Saxmund's day,
Ascends a knoll, as much are known in Suffolk's understated way,
Where to the right a noble church which flowers bright in season grace,
And to the left the Manor Farm that lichened trees embrace.
No more a landmark, Manor Farm, but round its meadows fair
Lie the remaining acreage of John Crisp, once its heir;
Here John sustains his livelihood, eggs from free-range hens,
He has no truck with batteries, cramped tortured fowls in pens:
His flock, Babcocks and Isabrowns, flutter free and roam,
Roosting by night in airy huts, unfettered make their home,
Free as the rooks that wheel above the gentle grass below
And eggs are brown and shells are firm, which clients come to know.
No longer young, when day is done, John goes to join his spouse
Where nightingales sing serenades by their bucolic house –
Excepting nights when wily fox raises a cackled alarm
And John with gun at half-cock waits to scare it off his farm.
And day by day, seven days a week, he tends his eggs for sale;
He feeds his hens and waters them, collects eggs in a pail,
Then modernised, rolls them through a gauge (by dexterity judged
                                        aforetime):
The radio plays, his car-borne trade buys fresh from his emporium,
Cheaper than supermarkets! and leave money in a tin.
That biscuit tin was stolen once by some light-fingered villain.
John nailed the next tin to the bench, the lid it had no seal;
Though he's no richer profit wise his customers don't steal.
            All this I have heard through the years when John feels
                                        loquacious.
Now Christmas comes around again and business is spacious.
I waited for his latest batch; John steadily muddily came
Accompanied by a large white goose, ponderous, touching and tame;
Close at his heels it waddled and swayed, a good twenty-pounder.
"Why Mr Crisp," I cried, "you've found a pet!" "A bounder,
A bloody nuisance, that's what," said he: "She hasn't any sense,
I moved her to the far field and she straightway flew the fence;
Follows me wherever I go, wanting to be friendly".
"You must make her your Christmas dinner then," said I with faintest
                                        irony:
      "No, that I won't," said John.

SHARDS

Porcelain girl, rose-petalled, unblemished,
With long long legs and discreet tattoo,
Shining in health, a life advantaged
In a birthright of Peace that's for millions taboo,
Divorcing on caprice, you take for granted
The assets of England served on a plate;
Lithe as a leopard, gym-strung and dieting,
Resorting to surgery to acquire chosen state.
One of the new generation of women,
Swift in riposte and sudden to leap;
Feminists anticipating back-stabs
Who answer to none and earn their own keep.
Has no one told you, loveliest lady,
Who deep in your heart craves what girls would attract –
The love of a soul-mate is still your ambition;
And men are romantic spite their macho act.
How can I tell you, a man needs to woo you,
The tenderness of woman is all he'll require:
So when you out-drink, out-swear, and out-sex him,
You unconsciously cancel your own heart's desire.

THE HERETIC

Satan sat at the Gate of Hell smoking a fat cheroot;
His features in the half-light fell Angelic,
Very like Gabriel, Michael and Raphael too.
Were they not brothers once awhile before Eden was new?
But now with narrowed eyes and sneer
The smeared resemblance was blurred;
"Running this earth's no sinecure," his attendant devils heard:
"So many applicants at my gate
Pleading preferential estate,
Excuses all, when it is too late,"
Said Lucifer akka Nick.
"Their game defines their Creator," he spat,
He bitterly spat, showering ash in a volcanic crater –

"That enemy at the Golden Gates
Demonstrated in chilling manner
What must befall his initiates
Who bear the Christian banner.
These chose my way, the easy way, the primrose path;
Yet now complain that my come-uppance is similar –
Only dated post mortem.
For I am King of the Underworld,
No flames of Hell – how juvenile –
Mine burn into the souls of men,
Not cleansing coals but putrescence vile.
For Hell is a serial replayed video, a recurring tape, to edify
These dregs who must watch how their confrères maimed
To attain our demonic company.
Comparing notes is their desert –
How did you inflict such hurt?
And I, and I, the same.
Oh, they shrivel as aeons go,
Penned to their relentless show,
Lost, along with me."
And a tear ran down his cheek.
"For I am what I am."
And he brushed aside his thirst for love,
And turned his back on the light above,
And muttered "Pray for me."

TO A DEPARTING BROTHER

We came to a parting of the ways
And all not said unsaid,
Dimmed by memory's glaze;
For both a life ahead,
You to that unplumbed land
Whose dreadful shore you stand
And I uncharted and alone,
My lodestone gone.

CASTLE MALL

The castle spoke from his grassy mound
As he watched the hole in adjacent ground:
My hill was made by serf with spade,
Shovel and barrow – no bulldozer's aid –
By labour it grew, by backache and callous,
Sweat and shiver and foreman's malice
And Normans' pittance for Saxons' toil,
Erecting their monument on English soil.
The castle sighed as the Park and Ride
Bus brought more tourists to peer inside
The museum, toss coins in his bottomless well.
Said the time-honoured castle, I could tell
Of how horsemen approached my moated gate
And torches advanced processions of state
And noble children sported and grew –
Times changed with them, with circumstances new –
I have seen terror, executions on gibbets,
Famine and fire and dungeon's secrets.
Four-square I stand and regard this Mall
Spring from my side – knapped flint withal –
Electric lights and powered cars,
Sheets of glass and rich bazaars;
And I dream of a thousand years now past
And wonder at progress and think – will it last?

THE WITCH

She is a witch, they said,
You can tell, they said
By the way she stares into space
And mutters.

Leave her be, they said,
Don't go near when you yell,
Children, she'll cast a spell –

31

Hark how she stutters!

She lives alone, they said,
No friends, her husband's dead
If ever she was loved, they said.
Not that it matters.

Perhaps she's mad, they said,
With her goat and her cat to bed;
She only goes out by night
In rags and tatters.

She picks toadstools, they said,
In woods, and nuts and berries
And twigs to fire her pot
And stir her gravies.

One day they'll find her dead
In her filth and hunger,
And burn her shack to the ground,
A threat no longer.

EAST ANGLIA IN WALES

Thither I come now, in the summer weather,
Now will I prove to myself the travellers' tales:
Purple are your vistas, but we too have heather;
These then your mountains – this is your Wales.

Lovely are your mountain streams, leaping to the valley,
Shouting wild cadences with springs from bedded rock;
I love a land where the level rivers dally,
Tranquil our peace without the rushing waters' shock.

Roughshod go your mountain roads, riding up and down hill –
Hills that challenge heaven and mock its many moods,
Grey with infertility, in their hauteur hostile;
I will content me with the green air of the woods.

Your winds for ever lick the flanks that ever stay unaltered,
Whose rowanberry trees are fey with Celtic fires ablaze;
With their cloud gowns chilly your heavy heights are haltered,
And lack the brittle champagne air of our clear August days.

Oh high hills carve the skyline and comb the white clouds'
      tresses,
They dim into the distance with ancient symmetry;
But the mist-mantled mountains are mute in their fastnesses,
It is the marsh and meadowland that will commune with me.

NIGHT DRIVE

Passing, passing, fading, dying,
The twin red lamps of passing cars –
Winking blinking, interweaving,
Glowing, growing, yellow stars.
People coming, people going
In their caul-like metal cans,
Now departing, now halloing,
Controlled clearway, cat's-eyes showing,
Following their ordained order,
Driving to their several plans.
People, people, men and women,
Little children strapped in seat –
Faster, faster, through the gloaming
Faster than the fastest feet.
Lights are quick, but thought is faster,
Faster still man's body flies
Hurtling with the yellow headlamps,
Only leaving twin red eyes.

CANDY

"Handy-Pandy sugardy candy, French almond rock" Nursery rhyme.

1. White sugar mice girls
   With chocolate drop babies
   Parading the High Street
   Pushing their prams,

2. England's new faces,
   England's new accents,
   One more facet
   Of the Mother land.

3. Pity the granddads,
   Humbugs and peppermints,
   Look-alike Alf Garnets,
   Colonel Blimp clones,

4. Orphans of the Great War,
   Brothers lost in last one,
   Prisoners in Burma,
   Hungry for home:

5. Home with the nightingales,
   Mackintosh's toffee,
   England, green England,
   Land of the free,

6. Bringing in the lost ones,
   The refugees from tyranny,
   Liquorice allsorts
   For afternoon tea.

7. Spare a thought for granddad,
   Clove balls and cough drops,
   Born to an Empire,
   England the crown;

8. Youth spent in colonies,
   "Bring a gin sling, boy,
   Of course I like the black man,
   Apartheid I disown"

9. "But they haven't any culture,
   Music, literature,"
   Dentures crack
   On aniseed balls.

10. Up and down the High Street
    See the many faces,
    Kaleidoscope of colour,
    Candy fluff stalls,

11. Sweets in the melting pot,
    Stir them all together,
    Mixed fruit pastilles
    And sugared true hearts:

12. England absorbs them all,
    England is richer,
    Sweets taste sweeter
    When prejudice departs.

HOMECOMING

A bird beat on the window in that night of rain,
An owl shrieked from the tapping trees
Like some soul lost in pain.
The clock chimed thirteen as I waited, waited;
I counted, as I waited for the wheels to usher you in.

A flower fell from the mantel vase
And a picture slipped – was it air
That made the coals collapse? Then a step
Hollow at the entrance stair:
You paused beneath the lanterns
With their yellow oily glare –
And I saw before I fainted
That you cast no shadow there.

THE LANDING OF COLUMBIA

They were men.
Hard sinewed, calloused hands,
Spread sandaled feet,
Running their little ships, their flimsy craft
Over the shingled sands,
Out, out into the breakers and beyond,
Embracing open sea with oar and sail.

They were men in prime of life;
Honed flesh withstanding gale
And bitter water and the great green depths
To mount an alien shore.
Men were they, wading into the hostile glare
Of wary strangers guarding their home ground.

Besotted men, they came, by Christ in thrall,
And Peace! they cried, we come
Neither to rape nor plunder. See, we bear
No other weapon than the craftsman's awl.

35

Peace, peace! they cried,
We bring Christ, our brothers, come to Him,
Come, know your God and King!

SAILING SONG

The reeds lean to the breeze,
They sway, crackle and sway;
And the breeze plucks notes
From their multiple throats,
Till a whispering song, like a lullaby's hum,
From the rustling reeds is blown.

The water laps at the reeds,
It slaps, plops, laps with the flood;
And the lap, lap, lap throbs a sleepy beat
At the feet of the reeds in the mud.

The boat heels over and skims,
It slices the water with sound;
The sails are set and the pilot honed
Till craft and helmsman are one.
In the wake of the wash
Of the boat's fleet run,
The moorhens dart to their reedy home,
And the boat, and the beat, and the whispering song,
Are together reflected in broken light
Split by the waves that slap and are gone.

THE PINING SWAN

Two noble birds at dawn of day
With scarce a ripple in their wake,
Glossy and white with ebony beak,
A touch of colour on each cheek,
In close communion dip and sway.

Two royal swans, a partnership
Of twinned content, idyllic scene,
Since his first adolescent preen
And her compliance to display;
They were a pair for life, to shame
Couples whose faithlessness demean.

Together trusting, they approached
The human youth intent with gun:
Such power to hand, such deadly fun,
To shoot and kill whate'er had life.

He had the first swan in his sights,
A target sure, an easy prey,
A trigger pressed, a shot, a splash;
And then the miscreant ran away
Perhaps appalled by what he'd done.

Who can translate a moron mind?
Blood streaked the victim's limp reflection,
He floated, all sensation gone.
The desolate mate, not dead but stunned,
With piteous grief his corpse pursued
And stroked against his lifeless form
Already sinking.
Till in abandonment subdued
And finally comprehending death,
She bowed her lovely head in pain;
And from that day no longer came
For food, but clearly weaker grew.

And when three weeks in sorrow passed
She laid her loving head along
Her wasted back and breathed her last;
To pair, perhaps, in Paradise.

SONNET: DEATH OF A SUBMARINER. BARENTS SEA

Olga, I love you. Do not grieve for me
Entombed beneath this cold relentless wave,
All hope abandoned, help denied, and dark;
With buried comrades sealed in waxen grave
The breath of death brushes my rigid brow:
This searing heartache we together share,
Knowing we shall not meet again my love,
Olga, my wife – this pain we both must bear.
Wash it not with tears, nor let the ache
Of sorrow blind those memories of delight
That cannot be erased. A dawn will break
Beyond this pit of grief: and glowing bright
On that far shore, no longer desolate
But rapt and entire we merge inviolate.

THE COUNSELLOR

I am a Counsellor, a Counsellor no less,
You might assume on seeing me I lack the right finesse?
A tad immature perhaps? Short skirt, stiletto boots
And glasses square, but never ever judge by people's looks.
I have the Qualifications, proved by my degree
Hard won by three years' graft in Sociology:
Three modules retaken, but I got there in the end
And I know humanities' vagaries and the messages they send.
My line entails the right approach to each genetic mindset –
Eye contact, tender touch not overdone – don't call old ladies 'Pet'–
Your feelings must reflect concern, it's simple empathy;
And the work is not all easy, clients resist or stay
In denial far too long and fight the urge for tears.
I have to curb impatience with those of senior years.
A full hour's my limit. All some want is babying!
There comes a point when the patience of a saint wears thin.
Some would you believe want prayers –
That's not my line, I leave that to the carers,
Parsons and the like, a funny lot who call

With no serious empathy that I can detect at all;
There's one walks in without a knock and lumbers to a chair,
Bangs out his pipe and says – can you imagine? –
"That's a fine pelargonium, planted perhaps by Jim?"
"Yes, yes," the client cries and weeps and makes him tea.
How that can pass as Counselling is way beyond me.
So I see the seamy side: four cases a day at least;
I repeat I earn my salary. I know one who's a beast:
"Wait till you've suffered," said this cow, "then you can counsel me!"
I nearly swore at such ingratitude and vanity.
I've lost my granddad and my Nan and broken with my steady,
So I've run the gamut of misery in my short life already:
However, that's a Counsellor's lot. Better than nursing or teaching,
Couldn't stand kids or bedpans. At least Counselling's not demeaning.

A HOLIDAY

On a high in June,
With the heat-haze muffling the horizon
And sunlight illuming each leaf,

My son made me a holiday in his new Montego,
His blue Montego,
His Montego diesel-powered.

Strapped in the carriage we sped away,
No route designed, no time decided;
Only the sea our destination,
The sea on the Lincolnshire coast.

For where else would you head in summer?
No mountains in Lincolnshire.

And as we went we discoursed on this,
We conversed on that,
Until in Horncastle the market beckoned
And sweets displayed unhygienic drew us.
Liquorice.

Then coffee in a caff.
On a June day in the Montego we gorged on liquorice.

And the fields rolled by.
Acres of flax, blue as Mary's robe;
Rape's blistering yellow;
Then buttercups softly gold.
Fields of beans, scented, grey-green
And tender young peas in fresh leaf:
And all about the rippling grass, the June grass, the hay to harvest.
Lord! what a lovely land.

And at length the flat fields flattened further,
The trees spaced wider and grew stunted,
The sea air welcomed us.
But not the sea!

The Lincolnshire sea is elusive.
It lies beyond sand flats
And mud wastes where men gather cockles.
It drums with the roar of traffic
But you see only the white wave line.
Rivers lead to the sea and sluices control their flow
With weird names like Black Gowt, Ferriby Sluice, Pode Hole.
We looked at the rivers and fishermen
But the sea we only heard.

Yet pubs a-plenty.
Pie and peas and lager and home via Louth.
Louth with its pinnacle of spire.
Louth with the spire climbed in legend.
Louth with the tale of a child from the sea
Who became its citizen of substance.
Louth gave us tea in a tea-room, No Smoking,
And we drove home content from a holiday in Lincs.
My son and I.

Home we went –
Only pausing to study one more lock,
        Of antiquity, called Ticklepenny.
        Home content.

THE SWALLOWS' EXODUS

The swallows are circling,
Scything their sections,
Carving their arcs
And cleaving the light –

Free of restriction,
Cloudily cushioned,
Beadily feeding,
Living in flight.

Songlessly whistling,
Leading their fledglings,
Instinctive aeronauts
Diving in space,

Drawn by the mystery,
The calling, the longing,
The impulse to abandon
Their mud-bound birthplace.

Pulled to the summer-land,
Heat blazing Africa,
Away from the winter
And hard frozen earth,

Families, neighbours,
A whole population
Seized by an urging
Implanted at birth.

See how the shadows
Of swallows assembled
Scribble graffiti,
Momentum defined,

Small feathered miracles,
Shafts of endurance,
Concerted by thought
In their Creator's mind.

DANCE OF DEATH

They rape young virgins in Bosnia
 And mutilate young boys,
Prisoners die of worse than wounds,
Please send their orphans toys.
For we are the mealy-mouthed men,
The leaders of nations once great,
And before we act we must confer,
Meet and discuss and debate.
Let's consider all sides of the question,
Let's count the cost if we move,
Let's call a quango and dance the tango –
Busily static – so what can you prove?

Let's keep our seats safe in the Commons –
An election's yet to win –
And our prime aim is to stay the same
And neatly save our skin.
The People are all behind us,
They'll forget our little tricks
By watching horrors second-hand
While the Lottery gives them their fix.
So let us waltz while we play them false,
Yesterday's news never sticks.

For we are the Noble Nation,
We care for baby calves
And climb up trees to save birds and bees
And strike for more pay in the fat-cats' way
And exclaim at sleaze in tabloid journalese –
    So knees up knees!
    Bosnia's not in our backyards.

THE WARRIOR: ETHNIC CLEANSING. (KOSOVO CIVIL WAR)

He herded them into their house, their happy home
So hardly earned, so dearly bought by back-break years of toil;
Wife, children – ah, that pretty babe! – creased age
And neighbours, friends of seasons' comradeship,
All fear possessed, all paralysed by fear.
One armed man, drug inflamed,
One thought alone, to kill, delete, destroy.
Oh, history is rewritten in that hour:
Again the Nazi, Vandal, Goth – such hate, such bile –
Again this wretched world sees Satan win.
Blood, brains, entrails explode, limbs lacerate and cries
Unworldly, piteous, shriek their Calvary.
He walks away sated and confident
To live, to live;
Lies with his wife and lulls his pretty babe
And must not think.
He lives, while shrieks resound as children play:
He lives, and will not look or think or sleep.
His gun lies idle.
He lives.
He lives,
Lives,
Lives.
Then dies.

MAN IN A HARD HAT

He came to my door on a Friday,
Neither servile nor overly bold,
A burly man in a workman's hat
Doing his duty as told –
Courteous and solemn, 'Ma'am, it's off your telephone
Till 4 p.m. at earliest,' in a voice of Irish tone.

The burr and caress of a Dublin sound
And its timbre spanned decades in one bound

To a voice I broke my heart over,
A voice that never knew fleshly lover,
Yet scarred my soul with desire so strong
It marred my waking hours seven years long.

THE STYX

Stand on the brink of the water,
Watch the waves lap the brim
Where the green depths swallow the shadows
And grey spume eddies a hymn.

Rolling for ever the river –
Too late to restore or defend –
Dropping us deep in the current,
Drawn pre-ordained to our end.

So I stand, wet-foot and weary,
Waiting to shed tired toils,
Releasing the bonds of yesterday
Into the river's coils.

THE PATRIOT

This is the land I was born in,
This is the land I love;
Earth of the earth of my fathers,
Home for the thousands that rove.
Nurtured, fought for and dreamed of –
No son could love mother more;
With its meadows my dust will mingle
And my soul shall encircle its shore.

GRADUATION DAY

So young, these newly honoured adults.
Lovely, whate'er the form; the patina of youth
Paints beauty's bloom, firm limbs and springing step
And the smile of accomplished study now rewarded.
Savour this day. Absorb it, nor forget your present elation.
Seal this in your heart, a breastplate for the coming time.
Your life's future awaits; you are not insured
Against the vagaries you shall encounter.
There will be other joys. Love, a child,
Success, promotion, wealth; but, as inevitably,
Loss, heartache, pain, for this the lot of all.
Meet each day as it comes; hold in your heart
This happy day, yours for a passing hour.

IN THE MOOD

Bowling on the autobahn
In my grandson's jalopy,
Heavy handling wagon
Hundred twenty on the clock;
Vast vintage vehicle
Inherited from father,
Big car, blue car, pride and polished own car,
First-time owned car, earnings won:
Designer-stubbled grandson,
Graduated grandson,
Tee shirt, trainers – no earring, bonus plus –
Ferrying his granny
Beccles to Peterboro',
Jazz fills the jalopy,
Break tapping feet;
Syncopated journey,
Throbbing through the morning,
One and two and three and hiccup the beat:
Where have I heard it?
Far far far away,

Another life flickering,
Long long ago –
Uniformed young men,
Short back and sides men,
Haze of beer and cigarettes,
R.A.F. blue.
Conscripts and volunteers
Fighting for survival
Dance between the sorties
In the annexed club;
Boys slicked with Brilcreme,
Girls preening Victory Rolls,
Seize the pulsing moment
In the dusty Hut
Harbouring homesick nineteens,
Hardened men of twenty,
Wings on lapels, shining shoes and open necks.
I can hear the metre now
With my failing hearing,
From afar the tread of feet
On the wooden floor;
Band on the platform –
Drum – sax – was there a trumpet? –
A-rock with the rhythm of sweating beat.
Pick your partner, dance then,
One and two and three now,
Turn, swing and step it,
Reverse and sway and hold it,
Stamp and turn and twist it,
Rock, reverse and round again,
Hesitate between:
Dance across the century,
Tune through the century,
Gasp and hug your partner,
Steady on your feet.
In the mood, in the mood,
Belt it out again, band,
Take you partner's hand again,
In the mood.

Joyce Barton

Joyce Barton was born on a Suffolk farm in 1915. After her father's death in the First World War her mother had to vacate the farm but she still had the run of her uncle's farm and grew up with an abiding love of the countryside.

She trained to be a teacher at Norwich Training College and taught in schools in Suffolk before her marriage during the Second World War and the birth of her son.

After the war she followed her husband to East Africa where she taught in a variety of schools.

In 1965 she returned to England, teaching once more in Suffolk schools. Finally, as a widow, she came to live in Beccles to be near her daughter.

Joyce Barton has written poetry all her life.

ISBN 1-874739-31-5

£3.50

9 781874 739319 >